SHARKS

AN IMAGINATION LIBRARY SERIES

THE WORLD'S STRANGEST SHARKS

by Victor Gentle and Janet Perry

Gareth Stevens Publishing
A WORLD ALMANAC EDUCATION GROUP COMPANY

Please visit our web site at: www.garethstevens.com
For a free color catalog describing Gareth Stevens' list of high-quality books and
multimedia programs, call 1-800-542-2595 (USA) or 1-800-461-9120 (Canada).
Gareth Stevens Publishing's Fax: (414) 332-3567.

Library of Congress Cataloging-in-Publication Data

Gentle, Victor.
    The world's strangest sharks / by Victor Gentle and Janet Perry.
        p. cm. — (Sharks: an imagination library series)
    Includes bibliographical references and index.
    ISBN 0-8368-2829-1 (lib. bdg.)
    1. Sharks—Juvenile literature. [1. Sharks.] I. Perry, Janet, 1960- II. Title.
    QL638.9.G36   2001
    597.3—dc21   00-052248

First published in 2001 by
Gareth Stevens Publishing
A World Almanac Education Group Company
330 West Olive Street, Suite 100
Milwaukee, WI 53212 USA

Text: Victor Gentle and Janet Perry
Page layout: Victor Gentle, Janet Perry, and Scott Krall
Cover design: Scott Krall
Series editor: Heidi Sjostrom
Picture Researcher: Diane Laska-Swanke

Photo credits: Cover, p. 13 © Marty Snyderman/Innerspace Visions; p. 5 © Bob Cranston/Innerspace
Visions; p. 7 © Doug Perrine & Jose Castro/Innerspace Visions; pp. 9, 15 © Rudie Kuiter/Innerspace
Visions; p. 11 © Doug Perrine/Innerspace Visions; p. 17 © Avi Klapfer/Innerspace Visions;
p. 19 (main) © Michael S. Nolan/Innerspace Visions; p. 19 (inset) © Gwen Lowe/Innerspace Visions;
p. 21 © David Shen/Innerspace Visions

Printed in the United States of America

1 2 3 4 5 6 7 8 9 05 04 03 02 01

Front cover: Nostrils like curly ram's horns gave horn sharks
their name. These sharks' noses are super-sensitive to the
smells of the critters they munch with all those tiny teeth.

TABLE OF CONTENTS

Words that appear in the glossary are printed in **boldface**
type the first time they occur in the text.

IS THAT A SHARK?

Is this a picture of a shark, a sting ray, a skate — or a slightly overdone, dusty pancake with eyes?

Sharks can come in strange shapes and with unexpected faces. It's easy to make a mistake and confuse a sawfish with a saw shark, mix up sting rays with angel sharks, or say you saw a **chimaera** instead of a horn shark. You wouldn't be alone in making those mistakes.

Such mistakes are probably the reasons for sea monster stories. People from long ago might easily have thought they saw a sea serpent instead of a **frilled** shark, or a monster and not a goblin shark.

The face of an angel . . . shark. Angel sharks were once called monkfish or bishopfish, because their fins look like flowing robes. Most of their swimming is done with their tails, not their "wings."

HOW TO MAKE A SHARK

Sharks are **cartilaginous** fish. That means their skeletons are made of **cartilage** — the same firm but flexible stuff that stiffens your nose and ears. Sharks do not have hard bones the way other fish do. Some don't even have vertebrae or bumpy sections in their backbone. (If you run your hand down your spine, you'll feel bumps. Those are vertebrae.)

Instead of having scales on their skin, sharks have teeth called **denticles**. Unlike bony fish, sharks don't have gill covers, or **opercula**.

Rays, skates, guitarfish, and chimaerae are also cartilaginous fish, just like sharks. They are all similar enough that scientists say they are in the same class of living things.

Don't pet that fish: it has teeth on its skin! Throughout the shark's life, its denticles are replaced as the shark loses them. See the spots where this Greenland shark's denticles were?

WHO'S YOUR MAMA?

Some scientists think that rays, skates, guitarfish, and chimaerae **evolved** from sharks. If those scientists are right, sharks came first in history. Over millions of years, some sharks gradually changed enough to become entirely different kinds of fish.

So rays, skates, guitarfish, chimaerae, and sharks are related — a bit like you are to one of your great grandparent's great great aunts — but they aren't from the same family.

For example, chimaerae and horn sharks both are cartilaginous, have vertebrae, look quite similar, have **dorsal** spines, and walk on their fins at the bottom of the ocean. And yet, chimaerae are not sharks, because chimaerae have opercula, and they have a beak instead of teeth.

Chimaerae are named for mythical Greek monsters made of mixed-up animal parts. They're called rabbitfish because of their faces, or ratfish because of their tails. This one is called an elephantfish because of its nose.

WHAT'S YOUR NAME?

Is it a ray, a skate, a guitarfish, or an angel shark? Those four fish are even harder to tell apart than a chimaera and a horn shark.

Most rays, skates, guitarfish, and angel sharks live on the bottom of the ocean, sucking up worms and munching crabs and shrimp. But angel sharks usually swim with their tails, just like other sharks. Rays and skates "fly" through the water by flapping their very large **pectoral** fins.

Sharks have gill slits on the sides of their heads, just in front of their pectoral fins. Rays, skates, and guitarfish have gill slits on their **ventral** sections, or their undersides, beneath their pectoral fins. And they don't have tongues. Sharks do.

Spotted eagle rays live in herds of 100 or so, are 7 feet (2.1 meters) wide, weigh about 500 pounds (227 kilograms), jump high, and are strong enough to pull small fishing boats.

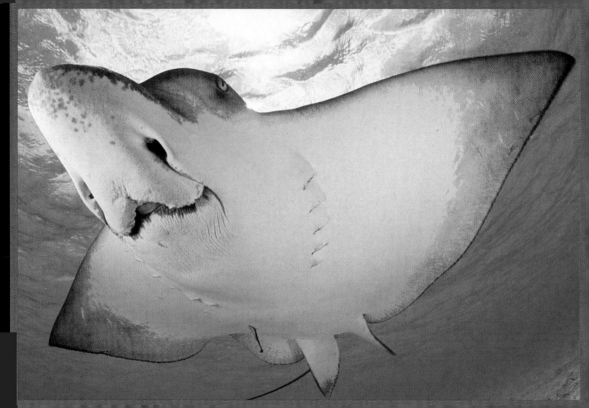

IS THAT A SAW YOU SEE?

It's even more difficult to know if what you're seeing is a saw shark or a sawfish. There are two ways to tell, though.

Like angel sharks, saw sharks have gill slits near their pectoral fins. Like rays, sawfish have their gill slits on their ventral sections.

They both slash the ocean floor with their saws in search of shrimp, crabs, and squid. But the sawfish's teeth are evenly spaced and sized, while the saw shark's are not.

Like some other sharks, but unlike sawfish, the saw shark also has long things that look like a mustache hanging from its saw. These sensitive mustaches are called **barbels**.

This long nose saw shark "walks" along the ocean floor near coastlines in shallow water, where it lives. The barbels help it sense prey — either by smell or by movement.

OLD-FASHIONED FRILLY GILLS

Many of the most bizarre creatures are called **"living fossils"** by scientists. The frilled shark is called a living fossil because it is so much like some **extinct** sharks that are found preserved in rocks.

Like ancient sharks, the frilled shark has no vertebrae. Its mouth is right at the end of its snout, and its teeth each have three points. Most sharks have their mouths under their snouts, and their teeth each have a single point. Frilled sharks' gill slits have little ruffles or frills. They almost look like opercula — as if the frilled sharks' great grand-parent's great great aunt might have been a **lamprey**!

Lampreys are wormy-looking fishes with toothy mouths. Sharks may have evolved from them.

The first set of the frilled shark's gills almost meet under its chin, so sometimes it's called a collared shark. Its teeth are also old-fashioned by shark standards. They have three points, not one.

HOW DO YOU USE THAT?

Hammerhead sharks, cookie-cutter sharks, and goblin sharks are three strange mysteries of the oceans. The ways they have **adapted** to their environments are unusual and not easily explained.

Hammerhead sharks have their eyes and "noses" on the ends of that strangely shaped head of theirs. Having eyes and nostrils further out from the center of their heads may give hammerheads a better sense of their surroundings. As hammerheads swim, their heads sweep back and forth so that they can get a full-circle view.

The hammer shape might also help hammerheads move faster through the water. From the side view, the "hammer" is shaped like the wings of a plane.

This scalloped hammerhead is at a "cleaning station," getting its mouth, skin, and gills cleared of **parasites** by king angelfish. Sharks even stop breathing to get their gills cleared.

MINI-MOUTH, BIG BITE

The cookie-cutter shark lives near the bottom of the ocean. For a long time, it kept a secret from scientists.

The cookie-cutter shark used to be called the "cigar shark" because of its shape. Then, someone noticed that it attaches its mouth to another animal, sucks the flesh between its teeth, and carves a hunk of flesh out of the live victim. Yikes!

The cookie-cutter shark is one of the most brightly lit fish in the ocean. Its body has a series of holes, called **photophores**, that glow in dark water. Scientists guess that these lights might attract food or scare predators.

The cookie-cutter shark got its name because of those teeth. The cookie-cutter's teeth overlap and form a small wall of teeth — like a blade. A cookie-cutter has snacked on this dolphin.

UNFINISHED WORK

The goblin shark looks like it was sewn together from mixed-up shark scraps! "Frankenshark" might be a better name for it.

Is the snout for shade, like a cap? No, the goblin lives in deep water, and it's dark there. Does the snout help it swim faster, like the wings of a plane? No, the goblin is slow. Is the snout used to dig up food from the ocean floor? No one can say for sure.

Maybe the goblin is on its way to becoming something else. Its long snout might be a step in **evolution** toward something like a saw shark, or a hammerhead shark . . . or something really odd.

It's fun to guess why all these strange sharks became as weird and wonderful as they are, isn't it?

Even though this goblin shark is dead, its long, sharp, curved teeth can scare you as much as a goblin in a fairy tale. But ocean goblins like this eat lobster and squid, not kids!

MORE TO READ AND VIEW

Books (Nonfiction) *Eyewitness Activity File: Shark.* Deni Bown (DK Publishing)
  Megalodon: The Prehistoric Shark. Dig and Discover (series).
   Stephen Cumbaa, and Susan Hughes (Somerville House)
  Sharks (series). Victor Gentle and Janet Perry (Gareth Stevens)
  Terror Below!: True Shark Stories. All Aboard Reading (series).
   Dana del Prado (Grosset and Dunlap)
  What Is a Fish? Science of Living Things (series). Bobbie Kalman and
   Allison Larin (Crabtree Publishing)

Books (Fiction) *The Escape (Animorphs #15).* K. A. Applegate (Scholastic)
  I Wish I Could . . . Swim with the Sharks. Gordy Slack
   (Roberts Rinehart Publishing)
  Punia and the King of Sharks: A Hawaiian Folktale. Lee Wardlaw (Dial)
  The Shark Callers. Eric Campbell (Harcourt Brace)

Videos (Nonfiction) *National Geographic's Really Wild Animals: Deep Sea Dive.*
   (National Geographic)
  National Geographic's Sea Nasties, with Leslie Nielson.
   (National Geographic)
  Vanishing Wonders of the Sea. (Sumeria)

PLACES TO WRITE AND VISIT

Here are three places to contact for more information:

Greenpeace
702 H Street NW
Washington, DC 20001
USA
1-202-462-1177
www.greenpeace.org

World Wildlife Fund
1250 24th Street NW, Suite 500
Washington, DC 20037
USA
1-800-CALL-WWF
www.wwf.org

Vancouver Aquarium
P.O. Box 3232
Vancouver, BC
Canada V6B 3X8
1-604-659-3474

To find a zoo or aquarium to visit, check out **www.aza.org** and, on the American Zoo and
Aquarium's home page, look under <u>AZA Services</u>, and click on <u>Find a Zoo or Aquarium</u>.

WEB SITES

If you have your own computer and Internet access, great! If not, most libraries have Internet access. The Internet changes every day, and web sites come and go. We believe the sites we recommend here are likely to last, and that they give the best and most appropriate links for our readers to pursue their interest in sharks and their environment.

www.ajkids.com
This is the junior Ask Jeeves site — it's a great research tool. Some questions to try out in Ask Jeeves Kids:
> *What are the weirdest sharks alive?*
> *Why are hammerhead sharks' heads shaped that way?*

You can also just type in words and phrases with "?" at the end, for example:
> *New shark discoveries?*
> *Sharks that glow?*

www.mbayaq.org/lc/kids_place/kidseq.asp
This is the Kids' E-quarium of the Monterey Bay Aquarium. Make postcards, print out coloring pages, play games, go on a virtual deep-sea dive, or find out about some marine science careers.

oberon.educ.sfu.ca/splash/tank.htm
It's the Touch Tank. Click on a critter or a rock in the aquarium to see more about it.

www.pbs.org/wgbh/nova/sharks/world/clickable.html
It's the Clickable Shark. Click on any part of the shark picture to find out how sharks work.

www2.orbit.net.mt/sharkman/index.htm
Enter the Sharkman's World near Malta. He's a scuba diver who is completely soaked in anything even a little bit sharky. You'll find poetry, music, and shark pictures there. The Sharkman is not a scientist, but he loves to talk sharks with other shark fans — like you!

www.pbs.org/wgbh/nova/sharks/world/whoswho.html
Here's a shark "family tree." Click on any of the titles, and you'll see what kinds of sharks belong in the same group, and why. If you see a picture of a shark you don't know, use the Shark-O-Matic to get answers.

kids.discovery.com/KIDS
Click on the Live SharkCam. See a live leopard shark and live blacktip reef sharks!

www.extremescience.com/creatport.htm
Click on Deep Ocean Creatures on the Extreme Science page, or any of the other choices at Creature World. This is a great site put together by a group of "Way Cool Scientists" about whom you can read here, too.

GLOSSARY

You can find these words on the pages listed. Reading a word in a sentence helps you understand it even better.

adapted (a-DAP-ted) — changed to better fit an environment 16

barbels (BAR-belz) — fleshy organs on fish snouts; they sense movement and smells 12

cartilage (KAR-ta-laj) — flexible but stiff support tissue, like bone but softer 6

cartilaginous (kar-ta-LAJ-in-us) — having cartilage for its skeleton 6, 8

chimaera (KI-mir-ah) — a cartilaginous fish, or a beast in Greek myths. The plural of chimaera is "chimaerae" 4, 6, 8, 10

denticles (DEN-ti-kulz) — tiny toothlike plates that cover a shark's skin 6

dorsal (DOOR-sul) — on the topside or backbone of animals or plants 8

evolution (ev-oh-LU-shun) — slow changes in an animal or plant over time 20

evolved (ee-VOLVED) — having changed gradually over time to fit surroundings 8, 14

extinct (ex-TINKT) — with none left alive 14

frilled (frild) — shaped like gathered cloth; the frilled shark has frilled gill openings 4, 14

lamprey (LAM-pree) — a worm-like fish that feeds on dead animals that have fallen to the ocean's floor 14

living fossils — animals that have changed so little over millions of years that they are almost the same as their extinct relatives 14

opercula (o-PER-qu-lah) — gill covers 6, 8, 14

parasites (PAIR-uh-syts) — creatures that live on other creatures, using their nutrients 16

pectoral (PEC-tor-ul) — around the area of the pectoral, or chest, muscles 10, 12

photophores (FO-toh-fors) — holes that glow in the dark on the bodies of some fish 18

ventral (VEN-trul) — on an animal's belly or underside 10, 12

INDEX